A BEACON BIOGRAPHY

Jennifer
LAWRENCE

Tamra
Orr

PURPLE TOAD
PUBLISHING

P.O. Box 631
Kennett Square, Pennsylvania 19348
www.purpletoadpublishing.com

Printing   1   2   3   4   5   6   7   8   9

A Beacon Biography

Big Time Rush
Carly Rae Jepsen
Drake
Harry Styles of One Direction
Jennifer Lawrence
Kevin Durant
Robert Griffin III (RG3)

Publisher's Cataloging-in-Publication Data
Orr, Tamra
    Jennifer Lawrence / Tamra Orr
        p. cm. – (A beacon biography)
Includes bibliographic references and index.
ISBN: 978-1-62469-001-3 (library bound)
1. Lawrence, Jennifer, 1990–Juvenile literature. 2. Actors–United States–Biography–Juvenile literature.   I. Title.
 PN2287.L28948O77 2013
 791.4302'8092–dc23
                                                                                    2012955645

eBook ISBN: 978-1-62469-012-9

ABOUT THE AUTHOR: Tamra Orr is a full-time author living in the Pacific Northwest with her husband, children, cat, and dog. She graduated from Ball State University in Muncie, Indiana. She has written more than 300 books about many subjects, ranging from historical events and career choices to controversial issues and biographies. On those rare occasions that she is not writing a book, she is reading one. Her four kids make sure she stays current on young and rising stars like Jennifer Lawrence, so she also watches a lot of movies.

PUBLISHER'S NOTE: The data in this book has been researched in depth, and to the best of our knowledge is factual. Although every measure is taken to give an accurate account, Purple Toad Publishing makes no warranty of the accuracy of the information and is not liable for damages caused by inaccuracies. This story has not been authorized or endorsed by Jennifer Lawrence.

Printed by Lake Book Manufacturing, Chicago, IL

CONTENTS

Jennifer Lawrence

Chapter 1

From Rejection to Nomination

Jennifer Lawrence is beautiful, young, and talented.

She loves to act.

So it was really no surprise that, like almost every other young female star in Hollywood, Lawrence wanted to be the girl that vampires and werewolves fought over and fell in love with in the movie *Twilight.* Eager to be cast in a film that was sure to be a huge hit, Lawrence read for the part of Bella Swan—and didn't get it. That winning role went to actress Kristen Stewart.

Lawrence was disappointed. Not getting the part, however, left her free to look at other projects. When she read the script for an independent movie called *Winter's Bone,* she knew what she wanted to do even more than play Bella Swan. She wanted the role of Ree Dolly, the main character in *Winter's Bone.* In an interview with *Hello!* magazine months later, she said, "I'd have walked on hot coals to get [the part]. I thought it was the best female role I'd read—ever."

It was a smart decision. Lawrence auditioned for and won the part—although she had to fight very hard for it. Critics loved *Winter's Bone,* and many reviews commented on the young, new actress who was able to make the character of Ree Dolly come

Lawrence's portrayal of Ree Dolly, a young woman struggling to save her family in a cold, harsh, and cruel environment, was profound and powerful.

alive on the screen. She was called a "modern heroine," and one critic said her acting skill was "a gathering storm." He added, "Lawrence's eyes are a roadmap to what's tearing Ree apart."

Soon, award nominations began to roll in from the Academy Awards (also known as the Oscars), the Golden Globes, and the Screen Actors Guild. One of these awards included an Oscar nomination for Best Leading Actress. It was a moment she would never forget—but at the time, she couldn't believe it.

In her parents' house there is a photograph of the important moment. "My mum has her arms up in the air, my dad's hugging me, my brother's clapping—everybody's happy. Except me. I just look aghast," she said in an interview with *The Telegraph.* Her family calls the photo, "The worst moment of Jennifer's life" just to tease her.

Certainly not being hired to play the role of Bella Swan was a disappointment for Lawrence. However, if she had gotten it, the role of Ree Dolly would have gone to someone else and Lawrence would not have become the second youngest person to be nominated for Best Leading Actress.

For Lawrence, there was no question that an Oscar nomination beat a vampire's bite any time.

It was hard to imagine that this amazingly beautiful woman on the red carpet of the 83rd Academy Awards was the same one who played Ree Dolly.

Chopping wood is a skill Lawrence already knew how to do before she began acting.

The role of Ree Dolly was one that Lawrence fit for many reasons. She already knew how to split wood, thanks to an uncle who had taught her when she was younger. "I went through a wood-chopping phase when I was nine or ten," she explained to *Rolling Stone* magazine. She knew how to clean guns because a cousin had shown her how. " [He] said, 'Anybody can spot a rookie right away,' and I didn't want that to be me," she told *The Jewish Journal*. "So I just carried around a cleaned-out gun, and got really comfortable with it." A hunter had also taught her how to skin a squirrel properly since she had to do it in the movie. What about the Southern accent? That was easy since Lawrence was born in Louisville, Kentucky, and everyone there had Southern accents!

When Jennifer Shrader Lawrence joined the family on August 15, 1990, she already had two older brothers waiting for her, Ben and Blaine. The three of them grew up teasing and playing jokes on each other. One of the boys' favorite tricks involved the family pets. "We had three dachshunds," explained

Lawrence in an interview on "The David Letterman Show." "(My brothers) put peanut butter all over my face . . . and then the dogs would do this [go crazy licking]."

Karen Lawrence ran a summer camp for children at the family farm while Gary owned a concrete construction business. Jennifer grew up riding horses and going fishing. She was a true tomboy. In an interview with *The Telegraph,* she said, "I was a really sporty child. I still like to win a race." In school, she was involved in many different sports, from cheerleading and field hockey to softball and basketball. She even played on an all-male basketball team and earned the nickname "Nitro" for her energy on the court.

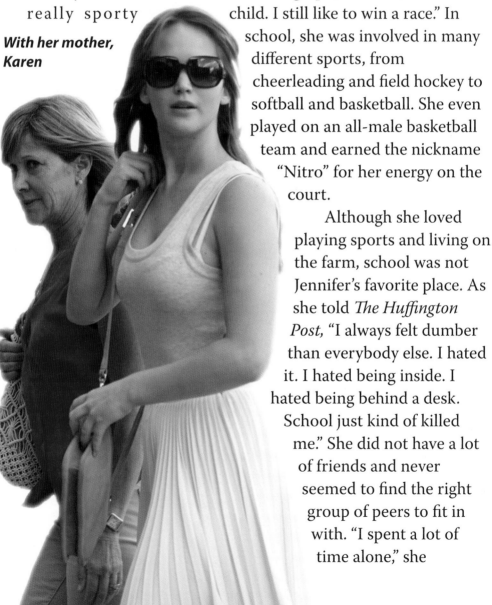

With her mother, Karen

Although she loved playing sports and living on the farm, school was not Jennifer's favorite place. As she told *The Huffington Post,* "I always felt dumber than everybody else. I hated it. I hated being inside. I hated being behind a desk. School just kind of killed me." She did not have a lot of friends and never seemed to find the right group of peers to fit in with. "I spent a lot of time alone," she admitted to *The Telegraph*. "My mum used to worry about me. She was prom queen, always socializing, and I never wanted to go to parties and that scared her."

A teen Jennifer in her school yearbook

It was not until Jennifer got the chance to play a shady character from Nineveh in a church play about the Book of Jonah that she realized something she truly was good at—acting. "This little extra just took over," her mother told *Louisville Magazine.* By the time Jennifer turned fourteen, she knew exactly what she wanted to do with her life—she was going to New York to become a famous film actress. Although Gary and Karen were proud of their daughter and cared about what she wanted, a career in acting was not what they had imagined for her. Their reaction to her news was less than thrilled.

"My parents were the exact opposite of stage parents," Jennifer admitted in a *Hello!* interview. "They did everything in their power to keep it from happening. But it was going to happen no matter what. I was like, 'Thanks for raising me, but I'm going to take it from here.' "

As she campaigned for the chance to go to New York, she found support where she least expected it—her older brothers. Jennifer told *Inquirer Entertainment,* "My brothers told my parents, 'You traveled with us for sports. You would be doing this if it were for baseball or football. This is Jennifer's 'sport' so you have to give her a chance, like you would give us a chance."

The Lawrences finally gave in. It was time for a trip to the East Coast.

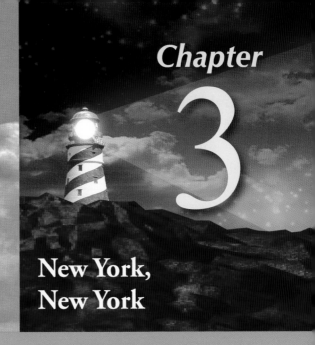

*Lawrence knew that
acting success was
waiting for her in
New York City.*

The story of what happened to Jennifer Lawrence while she was
in New York proves that sometimes fairy tales can come true. She
had moved to the city for one reason: to be discovered and
become an actress. And that is exactly what happened.

As Jennifer and her mother walked around the city during
the spring of 2005, trying to decide which auditions to go to first,
a man approached them. As Jennifer later told *Hello!* magazine,
"This guy was watching me, and he asked if he could take my
picture. We didn't know that that was creepy, at the time. So
we're like, 'Sure.' So he took my mom's phone number, and all of a
sudden all these [modeling] agencies are calling. And that's when
it all started."

At first, Jennifer was a model for companies like Burger King,
Abercrombie & Fitch, and MTV's *My Super Sweet 16*. Soon she
was also being called in to do readings for movie parts. Even
though she had never had any acting training of any kind,
Lawrence was completely confident. In the *Hello!* interview, she
said, "I never considered that I wouldn't be successful. I never
thought, 'If acting doesn't work out, I can be a doctor.' The phrase

'*if* it doesn't work out' never popped into my mind. And that dumb determination of being a naive fourteen-year-old has never left me."

Once Jennifer had a script in her hand, she was a natural. She told *The L.A. Times* , "I remember being in New York, reading a script, and I completely understood it. I knew I could do it. They were offering me contracts on the spot and telling my mom I was good. I was finally hearing I was good at something. I didn't want to give up on that."

Karen Lawrence was still not convinced that acting was the right career for her daughter. She did not entirely trust the judgment of the photographers and directors, wanting to protect her daughter from danger—and disappointment. Jennifer was determined, though. She told *Vanity Fair,* "I just kind of had this blind, stupid drive that really only a fourteen-year-old could have, of just knowing that it was going to happen. Well, not knowing it was going to happen—but just not really considering failure as an option. I just wanted to do it so badly. And I think my

Before New York, Lawrence appeared as Desdemona at the Walden Theater in Kentucky.

parents had never seen that in me before, and that made them take it more seriously."

With contracts coming over the phone and commercials giving way to movie and television parts, the Lawrences accepted the truth—their daughter really was an actress. They began taking her to as many auditions as they could in New York, including one for a role in a popular Disney television show—which she turned down. "[In one audition I was] asked if I could sing, and I was like, 'No. To be honest I don't think I'm a Disney kind of kid,'" Jennifer admitted. "When my parents picked me up, they yelled at me so badly. They were spending a lot of money giving me the chance to do this—and I had the potential to be on a television show that would obviously pay for everything and I was like, 'Nah.' "

At the same time, knowing that her future was going to be as an actress, Jennifer finished high school two years early by finishing her classes online so that she would be free to take any role that she wanted. Her parents were supportive, her face was becoming known, and school was behind her. It was time to become a superstar!

Lawrence became a familiar face on television when she played the daughter in the weekly comedy, The Bill Engvall Show.

From Silly to Serious

Looking over the roles that Jennifer Lawrence tackled in just her first few years, it is clear that she doesn't play just one particular type of character. She can act silly one moment and deadly serious the next. In one movie, she tries to understand her father's obsession with a hand puppet, and in another she is fighting for her life in a future world.

When Lawrence first began acting, she had small parts on television shows such as *Monk, Medium,* and *Cold Case.* Then, in 2008, her career raced ahead as she played in three movies. She had a small role in the film *Garden Party,* playing Tiffany. She also starred as Agnes in *The Poker House* and as Mariana in *The Burning Plain.* In this third movie, her costars were established actresses Charlize Theron and Kim Basinger. Lawrence stated to *Collider* that when starring with accomplished actors like that, "I always try to be a sponge and soak up as much as I can."

While she was making these movies, Lawrence was also seen weekly for three years on TBS Channel's *The Bill Engvall Show.* She played Lauren Pearson, the sassy, silly teenage daughter in a funny family. Viewers across the country saw her as a pretty, perky flirt—

THE *Hollywood* RTER

JANUARY 16, 2011

10 PAGES OF
THE GLOBES
The brutal fallout
from Ricky Gervais

Parties, gowns
and pictures

Rudin vs. Weinstein:
The rivalry heats up

THE INSIDER'S
FESTIVAL GUIDE
The breakout movies,
stars and players in
Park City and the new
rules of dealmaking

The
MAKING
of an 'IT'
ACTRESS
Passed over as Twilight's
Bella, JENNIFER LAWRENCE
fought to be in Sundance
hit *Winter's Bone*. Flush with
awards one year later, the
20-year-old shows how
starting small may be smarter

Photos like this made it hard to convince producers a cover girl could play a desperate heroine from the Ozarks.

and that made a real problem for her when she read for the serious part of Ree Dolly in *Winter's Bone*.

The producers needed a plain, gritty, tough main character—and Lauren Pearson seemed quite the opposite. When Lawrence auditioned for the role, she was turned down—three times. "I had to fight for it," she recalled in an interview with *The Huffington Post*. "I auditioned twice in LA and then they said I was too pretty. So I took the red-eye—which, just for the record, will take care of that—and flew to New York like a psycho and showed up at the New York auditions with icicles in my hair and was like, 'Hi! I'm back!'" Lawrence walked into the audition without any makeup, without washing or brushing her hair, and physically exhausted. "I think that once they saw that I had the exact kind of stubbornness and competitiveness that Ree has, they were like, 'Oh well, nobody else is going to be this stubborn and this crazy to embark on such a journey,'" she added.

To play the part of Ree Dolly, the producers changed Lawrence's good looks even more. They added a yellow polish to her teeth, pulled a dirty knit cap over her hair, and had her stop using any kind of lip balm so that her lips would look naturally dry and cracked during the months of filming in the Ozark Mountains.

Everyone who knew Lawrence was amazed at the depth of her acting in this movie, as she had to show enormous grief and fear—factors she had never faced in real life. "It was me, the girl from Kentucky with the wonderful family. Everyone was seeing this ability to go to this dark place that I didn't know that I had," she described to *Hello!*. "I've never been through anything that my characters have been through," she added. "And I can't go around looking for roles that are exactly like my life. So I just use my imagination. If it ever

As Ree Dolly

came down to the point where, to make a part better, I had to lose a little bit of my sanity, I wouldn't do it. I would just do comedies."

Lawrence's Oscar nomination for Winter's Bone helped get the young actress more offers than she knew what to do with. In 2011, she starred as Sam in the film *Like Crazy* and as Norah in *The Beaver*—with Mel Gibson and Jodie Foster. Foster and Lawrence quickly became good friends. "Jodie gave me hope because she's not only sweet and nice and great," Lawrence told *The Huffington Post*, "she's also the most normal and down-to-earth person. It's like

*Lawrence's role in **The Beaver** proved that she could take on many different roles. Although she plays a cheerleader, it quickly becomes obvious that there is much more to Lawrence's character than pom poms.*

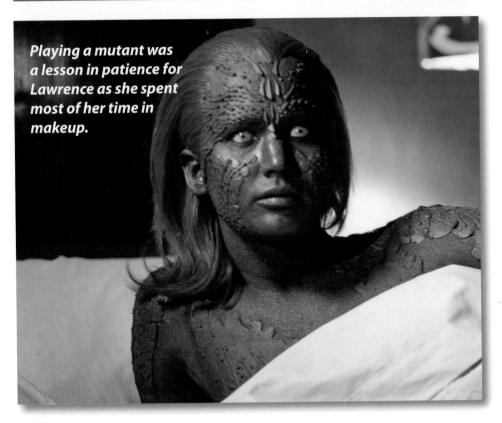

Playing a mutant was a lesson in patience for Lawrence as she spent most of her time in makeup.

she has no idea that she's famous. I remember looking at her and thinking, 'It can happen!'"

The same year, Lawrence left her plain image far behind when she played Mystique in *X-Men: First Class.* She spent most of her time in makeup: it took more than seven hours to apply her blue skin suit and three to take it off. "The platform shoes were the funniest part," she told *The Telegraph.* "But also, you can't move in 'em! We joked: the only thing [the suits] are is tickle-proof. Yeah, I can save the world and kill mutants, but I can't bend my knees to do up my own shoelaces." She became good friends with her makeup artists, and they passed the hours by watching *Sex and the City* movies together.

A flirty teenager, a determined daughter, a shape-changing mutant—what could be next for Lawrence? Perhaps it was time for a battle to the death!

Being cast as the main character in The Hunger Games *was exciting— and utterly exhausting.*

Chapter 5

Into the Future

In 2012, Lawrence was offered the biggest role of her life—that of Katniss Everdeen from Suzanne Collins's bestselling novel *The Hunger Games*. When she was offered the role, she was equal parts excited and scared. She told *Entertainment Weekly*, "I knew that as soon as I said yes, my life would change. And I walked around an entire day thinking, 'It's not too late, I could still go back and do indies, I haven't said yes yet, it's not too late.' "

Despite her fears, Lawrence took the role, and most reviewers believe that she did an amazing job. *Rolling Stone* wrote, "Lawrence reveals a physical and emotional grace that's astonishing" and calls her an "acting dynamo."

It was a challenging role to perform in many ways. Lawrence was trained in running, archery, climbing, and combat skills in order to play Katniss. Perhaps the most intimidating part of the role was that so many people had read the books, they were very familiar with the characters. Would Lawrence fit those images? As she stated to *Collider*, "Normally, when you're coming out with a movie, nobody has really seen the character before. You're just giving it to them. I'm playing a character that most people have already had in

Breaks during filming were often spent reading and relaxing before it was time to get up and run again.

their mind, and heard her speak in their mind and seen her. That's a scary thing to go into, knowing that so many people already have pictures or an idea of what your character is." Despite her fears, Lawrence did not disappoint her fans in any way. Many believe that she brought the character of Katniss to life straight from the readers' imagination.

What would be next for Lawrence? She was already slated to return as Katniss in the next Hunger Games movie, *Catching Fire,* in 2013. In the meantime, she could be seen as Elissa in *House at the End of the Street,* Tiffany in *Silver Linings Playbook,* and as the lead in *Serena.* Amazingly, she had worked on more than a dozen films in less than seven years.

By 2012, Lawrence had many plans for her future. "Yeah, I do have big ambitions," she stated in a 2011 *Huffington Post* interview.

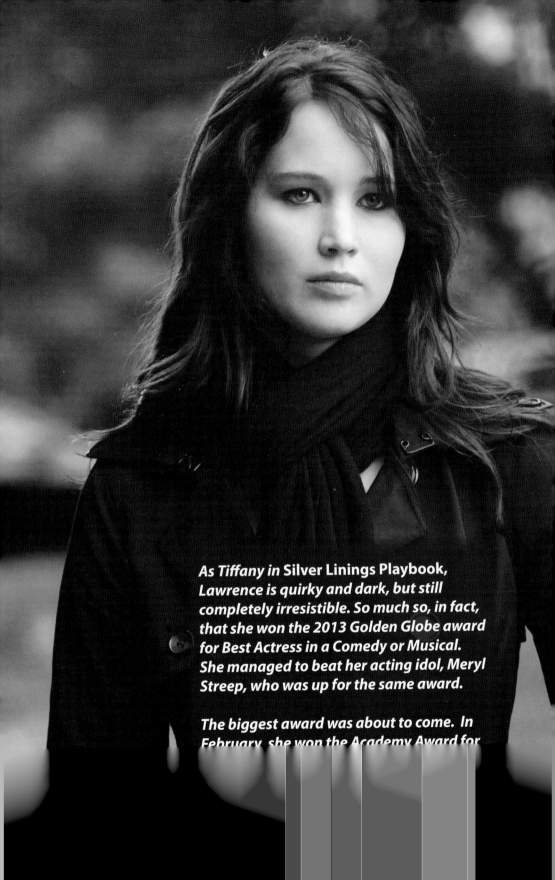

As Tiffany in Silver Linings Playbook, Lawrence is quirky and dark, but still completely irresistible. So much so, in fact, that she won the 2013 Golden Globe award for Best Actress in a Comedy or Musical. She managed to beat her acting idol, Meryl Streep, who was up for the same award.

The biggest award was about to come. In February, she won the Academy Award for

In summer 2012, while out walking her dog in Santa Monica, California, Lawrence (shown with her mom) saw a young woman fall to the ground. Without hesitation, she ran over to see if she could help. She called 9-1-1 and stayed by the woman's side until paramedics arrived.

"But I think we all do. I just want to keep working hard and being happy. When I think about myself in five years, sometimes I think about work and where I'll be in my career. But I normally just think about what kind of person I'll be. Will I be calmer or will I be more hyper? Will I learn how to listen or am I just always going to stay in this kind of nineteen-year-old zone where I could just keep talking forever? There are a lot of things that I know that I am going to learn about myself, because we all do."

Years ago, Lawrence sat at her school desk and wondered if she would ever be told that she was truly good at anything. Today, she knows the answer. As she said in an interview, "Knowledge is honestly everything. It's not just books and staying behind a desk and having a diploma. There's also traveling and knowledge about people and what I do and scripts and books. I'm very, very thirsty for knowledge. . . . Just because I'm good at something and have found success doesn't mean I'm done. I'm not even close to being done. I don't know if I ever will be done learning."

Jennifer holds her Oscar, wearing a gown provided by Christian Dior, the prestigious fashion house that has officially chosen her to represent their company's tradition in glamour.

1990   Jennifer Shrader Lawrence is born on August 15 in Louisville, Kentucky.

2004   She attends Kammerer Middle School.

2005   She and her mother stay in NYC to see if Jennifer can break into acting there.

2006   She graduates two years early from Ballard High School in Louisville. As it becomes clear that Jennifer has a blossoming acting career, she decides to move to New York City for good.

2007   She begins appearing in television series, including as a regular on *The Bill Engvall Show.*

2008   She acts in three major motion pictures.

2010   Winter's Bone is released.

2011   Lawrence is nominated for an Academy Award for Best Lead Actress for her role in *Winter's Bone.*

2012   She stars in *The Hunger Games* as Katniss Everdeen and becomes a well-known celebrity. She wins over critics yet again in *The Silver Linings Playbook.*

2013   She wins the Academy Award for Best Actress for her role in *The Silver Linings Playbook* and wins a Golden Globe for Best Actress in a Musical or Comedy for the same role. She is chosen as the new face of the fashion house Christian Dior. Lawrence stars in the film Serena. She joins the cast of *X-Men: Days of Future Past* to play the character of Mystique once again. The film is set for a 2014 release.

2006	*Company Town*
	Monk
2007	*Cold Case*
	Not Another High School Show
2007, 2008	*Medium*
2007–2009	*The Bill Engvall Show*
2008	*Garden Party*
	The Poker House
	The Burning Plain
2010	*Winter's Bone*
2011	*Like Crazy*
	The Beaver
	X-Men: First Class
2012	*Devil You Know*
	The Hunger Games
	House at the End of the Street
	The Silver Linings Playbook
2013	*Serena*

Books

Gosman, Gillian. *Jennifer Lawrence.* New York: PowerKids Press, 2012.

Krohn, Katherine. *Jennifer Lawrence: Star of* The Hunger Games. Minneapolis: Lerner Publishing Group, 2012.

O'Shea, Mick. *Beyond District 12: The Stars of* The Hunger Games. Medford, NJ: Plexus Publishing, 2012.

On the Internet

Daily news about Jennifer Lawrence

    www.jenniferlawrencedaily.com

Jennifer Lawrence on Facebook

    www.facebook.com/JenniferLawrence

Official Web Site of Jennifer Lawrence

    www.jenniferslawrence.com

Works Consulted

Balfour, Brad. "Best Actress Nominee Jennifer Lawrence Heats Up *Winter's Bone.*" *The Huffington Post.* February 25, 2011. http://www.huffingtonpost.com/brad-balfour/best-actress-jennifer-lawrence_b_828059.html

"The David Letterman Show," March 21, 2012. http://www.youtube.com/watch?v=RQczVqBT27o

Dillon, Nancy. "Jennifer Lawrence Rushes to Help Unconscious Woman." *The New York Daily News.* June 26, 2012. http://www.nydailynews.com/entertainment/gossip/jennifer-lawrence-rushes-aid-woman-collapses-front-santa-monica-home-article-1.1102537

Diu, Nisha Lila. "Jennifer Lawrence: 'The Hunger Games' Could Happen." *The Telegraph.* March 4, 2012. http://www.telegraph.co.uk/culture/film/starsandstories/9118903/Jennifer-Lawrence-The-Hunger-Games-could-happen.html

Eells, Josh. "Jennifer Lawrence Enters Oscar Country." *Rolling Stone.* February 8, 2011. http://www.rollingstone.com/movies/news/jennifer-lawrence-enters-oscar-country-20110208

Lee, Chris. "Is Jennifer Lawrence Going Stir Crazy from 'Hunger Games' Hype?" *The Daily Beast.* March 23, 2012. http://www.thedailybeast.com/articles/2012/03/23/is-jennifer-lawrence-going-stir-crazy-from-hunger-games-hype.html

Mock, Jennifer. "Celebrity Biography: Jennifer Lawrence." *People Magazine.* http://www.people.com/people/jennifer_lawrence/biography/0,,,00.html

Nepales, Ruben. "Why Jennifer Lawrence Is Less Confident Now." *Inquirer Entertainment; Philippine Daily Inquirer.* March 17, 2012. http://entertainment.inquirer.net/33847/why-jennifer-lawrence-is-less-confident-now

Pfefferman, Naomi. "Q & A with Jennifer Lawrence of *Winter's Bone*." *Jewish Journal*. February 13, 2011. http://www.jewishjournal.com/the_ticket/item/q_a_with_ jennifer_lawrence_of_winters_bone_20110203/from_the_ozarks_to_the_oscars_ debra_granik_of_winters_bone_20110127.htm

Radish, Christina. "Jennifer Lawrence Talks *The Hunger Games*, the Mall Tour, Director Gary Ross, and More." *Collider*. March 12, 2012. http://collider.com/ jennifer-lawrence-the-hunger-games-interview/151332/

Smith, Krista. "Jennifer Lawrence Talks about the *Winter's Bone* Awards Buzz." *Vanity Fair*. December 13, 2010. http://www.vanityfair.com/online/oscars/2010/12/ jennifer-lawrence-talks-about-the-winters-bone-awards-buzz

Travers, Peter. "*Winter's Bone*." *Rolling Stone*. June 3, 2010. http://www.rollingstone. com/movies/reviews/winters-bone-20100603

Unknown. "Jennifer Lawrence." *Hello!* Undated. http://www.hellomagazine.com/ profiles/jennifer-lawrence/

GLOSSARY

aghast: shocked or amazed

audition: to try out for an acting, singing, or dancing role

dynamo: a person full of energy and enthusiasm

heroine: a female hero

indie: a movie made by an independent company instead of a major studio.

naive: innocent

nomination: to be considered for a position or an award

red-eye: a flight usually between the hours of midnight and 6 a.m.

tomboy: a girl who is more interested in the traditional fashion, activities, and behavior of boys